Turning Radius

Douglas G. Campbell

Oblique Voices Press | Portland, Oregon

Turning Radius

Copyright © 2017 Douglas G. Campbell

ISBN-13: 978-0-9984446-0-4

OBLIQUE
VOICES PRESS

9310 SW 18th Pl
Portland, OR 97219

About the Author:

Douglas G. Campbell lives in Portland, Oregon. He is Professor Emeritus of art at George Fox University where he taught painting, printmaking, drawing and art history courses. His poetry and artworks have been published in a number of periodicals, and his artwork is represented in collections such as The Portland Art Museum, Oregon State University, Ashforth Pacific, Inc. and George Fox University.

The poetry in this book was written throughout the years before his stroke in 2012, which subsequently left him with a language disorder called aphasia. This book reflects the process of reengaging with his former poetry and also encouraging him to share his work with the world.

A dedication from the author:

For my wife, Rebecca: You are faithful in all things. You make me laugh. We go to Cooper Mountain. We walked on the beach, we talked about the moon and stars. We did things because they are beautiful. All things going and coming back. We saw big mammals gliding. At the moontide we could see the little boats. We could see up in the sky at another time, the spectacular moon. You are everything.

For my sons, Joshua and Ian: You support me. You work with me on saying sounds with words. You make me feel good about myself. You both feel good about yourselves. You are playful with me. You make me laugh. How can I say things that are beautiful. I love you both and I am proud of you.

Table of Contents

Lemonade Days

Canticles of Humanness

Turning Radius

Spirits of the Earth

Nature's Continuum

Listen to the Earth

On War and Art

Foreword

Douglas Campbell has been consistently creating art at a high level for over half a century. Though best known for his painting, printmaking, and fine work in mixed media, he has also pursued a productive life as a poet, chronicling that same impulse in carefully hewn language. *Turning Radius* attests to his years of dedication to that craft.

Rather than as a volume with a single formal or thematic focus, this book's seven sections coalesce as something more like an omnibus, or, on closer reading, like a jewel with seven facets, each of which displays a different aspect of Doug's rigorously lived inner life. "Lemonade Days" introduces the collection and is possibly the most typical for readers of contemporary poetry. Though stopping sort of the confessional, it offers the everyday situations, the personal struggles, the daily complexities which create the poet's need "to make a pocket for my soul."

The second section, "Canticles on Being Human," moves more deeply inward, becoming more elusive, more laden with psychological weight. It's darker, more imagistic, more dream rich in its retrospective shadows of inward landscape, as the voice shuttles between distance and intimacy. The eponymically titled "Turning Radius" makes apparent the book's philosophical foundation. The diction becomes more overtly Christian, the poems offer reflections on theology, on the insights of other Christian artists, occasionally in the masques of other characters. Here too it becomes evident that the voice is not only a poet and art historian, but a practitioner intimately familiar with the finite processes of making art.

"Spirits of the Earth" maintains the spiritual foundation but pushes beyond Christian language. The poems become more broadly vatic, and the prophet's words are rich in environmental awareness, rich with allusions to Native American thought, and rich in fastidious attention to nature: the earth itself is dressed as a character. This extension is furthered in "Nature's Continuum," with its more thinly mediated observations of nature, a minute detailing of natural landscapes with only an occasional revelation that a perceiver must be interacting with his world. Like Henry Thoreau, Campbell presents nature for its own sake without sacrificing the shimmering insights of careful attention.

"Listen to the Earth" reveals a world further removed from the pristine. Scenes portray the effects of husbandry or its antithesis–the uses and abuses of the human. Whether urban, suburban, or wild, the poems present the tenuous co-existence of humans and their no longer natural homeplace. Perhaps most effectively in this section, the masterful "Rainy Ridge" submerges the reader in an uneasy wilderness of time and dream, as hikers lose themselves in a not quite natural, not quite human landscape.

The book's concluding section, "On War and Art," embodies the harsher tones of the vatic voice. In the "war" portion, the vision is at times darkly cutting, almost apocalyptic, ugly. And the tenor pushes even to the section's "art" portion, which suggests a violence in the making of art–the frustration, the necessity, of cutting away: the best we can do at beauty, it suggests, does not come without material cost, even when intention is cutting "towards spirit." And like the material artist, in the book's penultimate entry "the poet spreads his smooth/and bitter words into a vast darkness." Maybe this isn't quite the conclusion we were hoping for: there is no escape into a present or transcendental sabbath. Instead, the book closes with a reminder that we are of the earth, we are bound to be human, there's no escape from human limitations. The final poem, "Wood-fired Torsi," changes this note:

Humans are "Born of fire/torn from the earth/scorched and twisted/is this second birth." Indeed.

Varied as it may be, this jewel with seven facets suggests an unsettling consistency, and that consistency is discovered in a complex of attributes that have characterized all of Campbell's artistic work: an attention to everyday details, startling in its intricacy; a sense of irony that laughs and rages but is slow to anger; a knowledge of natural phenomena that attests to many hours in the wilderness as well as in the studio; and a practiced craft that inevitably chooses the perfect form for the message conveyed. In this collection, a difficult longing for peace is wedded to a deep and holy anger: a rage that is saved from stridency by a kind heart, by a persistent attention to the sensual world and–when that sometimes fails–through faith in the God who created and sustains it.

William Jolliff
Professor of Writing and Literature
George Fox University

Lemonade Days

Itinerary

Are there foggy days, inside or
out, when you would desire a
large map of your life to spread

out on a table or a chart to
unroll across an empty lap,
complete with a red arrow and

the requisite words "you are here"
writ large? Or would such a
navigational aid be too revealing

of an as yet unwritten future
with its possibility of undesired
geographical complications

that you are not prepared to
face, with paths and roads
displayed? Or could such a

cartographic aid induce a
reverie seductively filled with its
unwanted enticements that

would lead you to skip ahead—
omit the now?

Routine

While I shower
small hands fumble to open morning's door.
Hands smear sleep from eyes;
unselfconscious yawns emerge
and recede.

Small voices begin
to ask the questions
with known and unknown answers.
Potties are filled.

Undressing is followed by dressing;
a white dog, or Lego blocks or a truck
clothe the hugs
the climbing into bed with Mommy.

Breakfast empties its bowls of cereal,
its cups of milk into mouths,
onto bibs and chairs and floor.
Potties are filled.

Then follows the unrest of the day—
games to play, groceries to buy,
lunch's sticky interlude.
Potties are filled.

Naps sometimes bring quiet
followed by reenergized play
until dinner's recharge.
Potties are filled.

Hand washing, teeth brushing,
more toys and running fill the darkening
before stories, prayers, songs and bed.
Potties are filled.

Looking Closer

With the rise of morning mist
when the sun draws for gray drapes
a lizard crawls on its suitcase
which changes color to match the sky
gray suited with a trout
collecting sequins in a brass bucket
to make a new bowtie
for a tadpole shifting his briefcase
with magazines on hydroponic gardening

in an eagles nest
car keys dangle on a fish hook
an oval oyster snaps closed
a salty golden brooch
which lives inside a photograph
of a mountain landscape watercolor

a snake surreptitiously peeks
into a dark dresser drawer full of silk gloves
worn only to green garden parties
held by a mellow cricket chirping only
to hide Beethoven on his stereo

I dip my hands into morning
and wring sparrows from mountain lakes to fly
I find a smiling oily otter
wound around my hollow toes
waiting for me to trim its mustache

Cloth

enmeshed
unable to disentangle
voices from my past, my present

my life is not whole cloth
where warp and weft interweave
order and design

snarled within endless tangles
hidden and lost beneath
packets of needles and spools

no loom to stretch
my twisted fibers
threads without end or beginning

send the sewer's hands
to stitch these strands
to make a pocket for my soul

Turning Around

Too many times
I have not stopped
to turn around,
to stoop
to bring into focus
some curiosity
clinging
to the edge of sight.

But this yellow patch
sewn into landscape of lawn
metamorphosing—
a wounded butterfly
climbing my extended finger,
delighting my young son
(who wanted to touch
this new creature - and did
so gently)—
led me to turn around,
to give up
for a moment the task
of picking up toys, chairs
and towels scattered on grass.

Journey to a Silent Sea

Last Wednesday
when the sky fell down,
and drenched my world
I sloshed back home
seeking heat and drought.
I unwrapped myself
while forming a small
kitchen lake amid the fake
tiles of the linoleum.

The linen closet beckoned me
and unrolled a large
towel into my waiting hands.
I enfolded myself
into this soft, absorbent
world and trundled
back to the kitchen, made
Darjeeling tea, then sat
at the kitchen table
lost in a haze of rising steam.

For some unknown duration
I sat and sipped unaware
of the world outside my
terrycloth cocoon where
cars sprayed pedestrians
as drivers aimed for the
deepest standing water as
they succumbed to the
mesmerizing influence of
wipers arcing before eyes
that looked but did not see—
or if they saw did not care.

I must have succumbed
to sleep, for I found
myself swimming through
the sky among the purple clouds
of Amangoor, where the
Marlin-like Netraxa soar
upward in great flocks
as the twin suns Belabeth and
Cabitha rise fraternally above
the forests of Denabore where
the Enkancari River flows into
the silent sea of Furicane Kaboor.

Tide Searchers

Heads tilting sandward,
backs bent slightly forward
searching.
A stiff irregular momentum,
small steps interrupted
by prodding toes,
by bending down
to pluck at shell fragments—
hoping.
Some carry sticks
with spoon affixed
for poking, digging
unmindful of sandstone cliffs,
unheeding of fringed waves—
wearing rubber boots and
parkas on sun-less days,
wearing T-shirts and
shoeless on rain-less days—
trudging,
leaving an ungainly,
temporary legacy on the shore
as an ocean swallows itself,
as tides recede,
searching among fragments
and rounded stones
for something whole.

Lemonade Days

On summer days when
the air slows to a crawl
and chocolate softens, melts
and spreads its sweet
aroma out to blend within
the heat-filled currents
that mingle with the oleander's
poisonous enchantments,
on days when dogs cease
to move as long as the sun
remains hanging in
that endless blue of sky,
inertia swallows the heart
and all becomes calm
and humid and lethargic.

On such lemonade days
when we lounged on
the cool concrete floor of
the screened-in porch
away from mosquitoes
in search of heat and blood
no real work could be done.
By late afternoon, after
the daily rain shower
the earth could only wait,
recline indifferently until
night began to bloom
and some notion of cooler air
began to dwell within us.
It was a time of deceit,
for the night remained warm
and tree frogs prowled

across window panes
searching for dinner, for
moths attracted, lured
by the feeble light of a
small lamp. The night
did not bring respite and
sleep came slowly as
damp hair curled and tangled
sheets absorbed perspiration
as white-eyed gardenias
sparkled and stars gleamed weakly
in those sweet and gooey
dark chocolates nights.

Assemblage

fused streets
traffic bumper to bumper
horns belligerently intruding

anger, frustration,
curses fill the interstices
of this metallic mosaic

each tessera radiating hostility
or crumpling inward
lost within emotional collisions

air bags protect from shards of glass
what keeps this hate at bay
what blunts this madness of our day

send in the flutes and clarinets
play tapes that soothe instead of stress
paint your boundaries in the air.

Abandoned

Empty coat hangers
rattle in my closet
where once
the honeysuckle
slept before the moon
humming birds wings
beat the settled dust
from unread books
sterile ghosts
on thin walkingstick legs
leave unseen footprints

Fathers' Words

Early that morning
before the day had been
picked apart by the
circling of crows or the
chickadees had searched
every branch of the
crepe myrtle, the son,
older now, wondered why
he had never read those
words, the ones in the books
his father once wrote.

It did not distress the son.
He wondered if his sons
would ever read the words,
he had stacked like cordwood
ready for the fire—the ones
hidden between covers
and shelved like row
upon row of tombstones.

Interrupted, by a diligent
towhee, scrabbling among
summer leaves inside the
closets of the ligustrum
hedge, his mind wandered
to other things—the aroma
of dinner cooking in
the cool kitchen, where
napkins unfolded like
seagulls and rose up
into the warm air to

disperse among clouds
riding the wind from
the western ocean.

Three Brothers

Three brothers climbing aboard life
ready to leave the known and
head out to somewhere else
far off. Like hot air balloons
they rise slowly into the cool
of morning, their bright, colorful
designs emblazoned like
logos on thin, synthetic fabric.

As morning builds towards noontime
the balloons drift over the green
hills and cross over the divided
highway, heading eastward
above the planet's slow spin.
Friends and other well-wishers
drift towards parked cars
after consoling the father and mother.

Since there are different dreams
lodged in the wishes the sons hold,
their paths diverge as they voyage
on currents of air. Soon they
can no longer see each other and
realize that the landscape
when seen from above, proves
unrecognizable, unknown.

Eventually, after hours or days
adrift, cresting on tides of air
each brother alights in some
likely place. As the years pass,
like pages turning in a novel
of adventure, each one spreads out

his life, returning only sporadically
to the launching site. They see how
the others have become different
or strange, less easy to know,
less easy to interpret, as though
a language shift has taken place
and the words they once spoke,
almost in unison, have given
way to argots filled with herbs
and spices—flavors that tease
or irritate the tongue.
The past they held in common
is lost now among the babble
of their individual journeys.
Only in the old stories do they
understand each other.

Lives unfold like worn maps
that in time tear along the creases
separating the gentle land
into uniform rectangles that
nobody knows how to reassemble
or reconnect. The desire to
return home, to find that nest
of long ago seems to fade
as tides rise and fall beneath
the moon. It is sad that brothers
need translators so that each
might speak his life clearly,
so that he might know again
the brothers of his past, his
playmates from so long ago.

Hollow House

The Emptying

Now that the house is empty,
now that the air is thick
with the smell of dust and mildew,
now that the drawers and closets
have been emptied of memories,
the cartons filled with folders,
sorted and reboxed,
ghosts have nothing to hold on to,
they lose their ever tentative grip
among these hollow spaces.

Now that the father lingers
on the edge of life, death,
now that the sons have come and gone
to the Mother's memorial service
and the furniture has been divided
and life drained from the rooms
the ghosts too have fled,
seeking some richer mausoleum.

The gardens too once filled
with camellias, bees, toads
and an occasional box turtle
seem to languish, almost desert-like,
now that the winds of death and illness
have sucked dry these empty rooms
so full once with family life.

The Mother gone now
wrenched violently and quickly from life
by a heart attack

disappears as drawers are emptied
and closets mined
for the gold she saved.
Some of the gold is real
much is fool's gold
that has lost its glitter.
As she disappears her life blooms
as memory replays the past;
and some of the past is new,
at least for her sons.
Her children's stories
written before her sons' memories
could hold them
bloom in their fingers.
Her wedding dress now yellowing,
beneath a note written to us all,
brought rain, the type of rain
that makes reminiscence flourish
and bear fruit.

The Weight

Death and the emptying of a house
bring more burdens
that may bury the living.
What should be kept?
What thrown or given away?
How much of the past can we bear
before our bodies or lives are crushed.
How many relics can we cling to,
at what point do we lose the present?

30 boxes filled with china
crystal, file folders, masonic swords,
stereopticon and slides

and toys all wrapped and taped
awaited the moving van;
they fill the corner where my father's desk
once stood. There he wrote articles,
revised books, in that spot,
typing with two fingers.

From that same typewriter came the funny poems
sent to each of us at Silver Lake Camp.
The seeds of love poems for my mother
popped open, sprouted and grew there too.

Letters to the editor,
were planed, sawn, and rebuilt there;
sentences praising good works
sentences condemning racism, greed,
political and moral stupidity.
The focus was crisp like ice,
the range broad and varied.
Copies of these verbal's darts, banquettes,
are scattered amongst the many leaves
that grew forth each new year
from that old Smith Corona;
leaves raked into files,
some more orderly than others.

Mother kept all of our letters,
underneath all she was an archivist.
Everything, or so it seems,
that we touched, wrote, drew, crafted—
if such a term can be used for
a second grader's ceramic piece—
was boxed or filed.
Years, too many years of memories
long forgotten, seep into the present,

making one wonder if among all this clutter
of mementoes the relies some key
to myself, my brothers.

Why did she not let go of this past,
why must we confront it,
confront the very humanness of it
with all its silliness, clichés,
middle-class banality, stupidity.

I throw much of my past away
saving a few tatters as mile posts,
more of the good
than silly or embarrassing.
From these remnants,
if I ever look at them again,
I can construct a quilt of my own design,
that better fits my image of myself.

Mother held onto these memories
more for herself than for me
far more for herself than for us.
Most of them have fled my brain,
but for her they were still crisp,
real, important pieces of her life.

Canticles on Humanness

Steel Mitten

though I am suffocating still
from the gaseous breath
of the cougar's sour snarl
I will drive my car into the sea
and leave it
on the hollow tongue of the gulf
on a salty spit
west of Indian Pass
I will make my own steel mitten
across from the island's oyster shells
and pottery slivers

on a later someday
I will visit rusting barnacles
and shake hands with hermit crabs
I will smile through my radiator
at the teethy shark mandibles
caught in my bumper
I will pack the upholstery
with scallops
 and recarpet with seaweed's
indoor outdoor shag

I will swim
back to the salty wind spit
to laugh with dead Indians
at archeological spiders
and sit with the fox
in the eye of a needle

The Salt of Dreams

hole torn into the mountain's green side
wound of darkness sewn to the grass

pit waiting for the blind wandering of sheep
vacuum pulling the silence of leaves from trees
sucking light from the particles of sun

well drawing my hands from pockets warmth
newborn fingers rushing to press the rock
nails scratching bundles of fine lines
upon a surface cold with the taste of ice
a skin textured with the flavor of stone

beams of carbide lick the deaf walls
my lungs exhale soft tongues of fog
ears capture the smallness of bats voices
wings and claws hug the darkness they know

stalagmites wait in the stillness of centuries
reaching upward toward the pulse of their twin
the breath of catacombs surrounds the air
among boulders arranged in cemetery darkness

thin stems of crystal are dressed with flowing mud
mineral tears drop from the weeping walls
drowning the shells of fossilized oceans
existence merges with the salt of dreams

Back Into The Dark Heart

Earth's stone cold feet
cling to a short life
just like any butterfly

flowered wings bloom
for several short days
only to shrink too soon
back into the dark heart

or explode into flames
against a windshield unseen

Carnival

We have becomes wizards of subterfuge,
hiding the mirrored faces we see
beneath makeup and lies—
we color our hair
polish our teeth
change the color of our eyes
retouch photographs
digitally enhance our images—
so others will not think we age,
grow weary or fall ill.

Death, we fear you more than ever
now that we live so long.
We deny the very bones within us
as we pump iron
flatten our abs
power walk our way backwards
toward birth;
we gorge on vitamins and ginseng
stretch our skin taut
with the aide of a surgeon's scalpel
so others will not glimpse
our battered and fragile egos.

Instead of faces we wear masks
that no soul can penetrate,
not even our own.
Our lips move, oozing pleasantries.
Our mouths open and close all day long
while our hearts are locked,
buried deep within vaults
beneath our pretence of youth.
We squander our lives,

we deface ourselves
as we run this race with death.
What vanity!

Embrace your wrinkled exteriors,
for they are your salvation;
in this nation of smooth talkers
they are a testimony
bearing witness to truth.

Enunciation

Collect the words
gather them in as they
swoop, swirl or drift.
The ether is overfilled
with pronunciation;
syllables are free for the taking.
rake up adjectives and verbs
bind up adverbs and nouns.
Eventually, when the air is asleep
when silence and emptiness
surrounds your ears, and
you need to shout,
then, if you have saved enough
you can unfurl them endlessly,
stitching sentences into banners,
regalia, tapestries, quilts—
give pattern and measure
to what otherwise would remain a mute,
unarticulated effluvium.

Requiem

For decades I have devoted myself to an austere
existence, similar to that of a pilgrim in the wilderness
as I searched through volumes seeking answers to
those questions others had posed, but for some
reason not worth pondering, they had neglected to answer.

I lived within libraries, surrounded by dust and
pomposity, submerged within a sterile sea. For
months my head was assaulted with such puerile
hurricanes of ignorance, countless dank skeletons of
proposals, bereft of living thought.   Cast adrift within
this ocean of indifferent and incoherent vastness, I
could easily have succumbed, allowing myself to
sink to the depths between purgatorial tides—currents
leading nowhere. My vision of some coherent
universal connections salvaged me, kept me afloat.

For there were buoys, though widely spaced, that drew
me onward to islands where other rational minds had
pointed, almost prophetically, towards some further
step—suggested, but not yet taken. Piece by piece
my model grew and prospered, no thanks to my colleagues
with their jeering eyes and whispered incantations
of doubt.   They had no vision, no persistence—
they married, took vacations and succumbed, each
to his or her chosen diversion, strayed from this narrow
path to truth I follow. Slowly, with great care and labor
I have addressed all contingencies, answered all questions
worth answering, until I am surrounded by great
palisades of thought resplendent—the work of my
own mind.   But now all I taste is dust and ashes, for I
find myself trapped within this inflexible perfection
that surrounds me. Enthusiasm for logic unbridled

blinded me to the need for passages. Others, who
might be impressed by this vast array of verticals and
horizontals, are barred access. And now that I
find my great universe of thought complete--each
concept following its designated track, each
particle of matter and anti-matter accounted
for, my neglected body, jealous no doubt of my
unrestricted mind, has tricked me and festooned each
muscle, each sinew with unendurable loneliness.

Rafting the River Styx

We had signed up for an underworld adventure,
so we should not have been surprised by the
septic stench, the roiling smoggy clouds that bit

into our skin like acid, etching pain into our
skin, tattooing us with our environment. Our
guide, a gnarled, wizened humanoid was anything

but garrulous as he plied his steering oar; he made
some attempt to avoid the bloated cadavers
afloat among pipes, industrial wreckage and small

islands of muck and ooze. With no warning he would
steer our creaking craft into a culvert, then into
some tubular channel within this tunneled realm,

and we would speed through darkness a-splash
with blood and offal, as white sightless insect-like
creatures dropped upon us from above and then

scurried across our faces toward some unknown prey,
until our tunnel and another intersected amidst a
churning broth barely visible within the circuit of our

lantern's feeble purview—attesting to the tossing
body parts within our tumultuous wake as some
new reeking aroma washed across our route. Through

a maze of underground canyons, passages of vast
dimension, we churned almost unable to breathe
in this substance, this carbolic ether of industrial

waste that sought to slither into our mouths, our
noses. It was a ghastly sightseeing trek that funneled us
through chasms crafted by our ancestors who once walked

the earth before us, and sent the unfortunate ones
to toil and die beneath the pleasant surface before
the sun sank within the carcinogenic miasma

they had brewed, they had spawned—their pathetic
and ill-formed monument to an unappeasable and
insatiable greed that devoured them and all they made.

Mountains Remember

Moon cold light
a dentist's drill
probing the mountains
grey granite molars

you will not find
my mountain's warmth
her black limber trees
will make a tangle
of your fingers
and pull from your chin
white dead hair

do not comb my mountain
with your icy winds
she won't take the kisses
of your flat
machine smooth eye

go search the city
there concrete coldness
will embrace your icy breath
as a magnet

cold clean city computers
already send you
shiny metal gift wrapped men
to lace the pours
of your dust face
with human trails

the earth
spit you out once

for your bitter taste
what my mountain remembers still
cuts like a bulldozer
through her heart

Night's Screamer

I have cut out the wind's tongue;
it would never stop babbling; in my ear
the endless obscenities of love.

This whispering tongue wriggles wormlike;
struggles in an empty wordless void
searching for a pair of worm lips hung
with lung sacked air below.

This severed tongue, night's screamer,
lies jailed between hooked fingers.
Empty sounds no longer tempt the silent brain,
ears no longer lunge at shallow breezes.

Stones Drained of Blood

Among round soft stones
somewhere stones
clinging to the moon's feet
silent stones

stones drained of blood

men of stone sucking cells
from tiny moss silvered songs
granite sucking sight
from black night's eyes

real dreams mix with corpses

the wind's sad witches
hide the sunlight
beneath the blind folds
of the bitter earth's ocean

sour brine pickled shrimp
pick the arrogant pebbles
from the sand filled brain

sift the weary silence
sort the dissonant void

beneath the heavy bloodless lids
filling the hollow jointed hands
I carry within my pockets
aborted sleep lies hidden

The Death

Elbows and chin protrude
from the dark throat of a steel bed

skin wrapped bones
gripped by purple fingered death
lie stiff with petrified marrow

old lives lie on death's tongue
waiting to be swallowed
begging to be digested
and lost

eyes sinking
closing back into their sockets' darkness
skin shrinking back

all life is pulled to the heart
still pumping

Well of Morning

I submerge my hands
into the deep well of morning,
I find a necklace
of woven goldfish scales
entwined about my neck
bracelets of tiny cricket feet
crawl up to clasp my wrist,
rings set with iridescent beetles
surround my fingers.
a breeze filled with birdsong
settles on my tongue
chipmunks dig small pits
grey warblers wrap the stiffened corpses
many small victims of sour dreams
lost within a lupine shroud

Beneath The Cat's Sleeping Eye

Wailing sirens bite my afternoon
solitaire cards fall upon dry hands
dripping words swallow my pen
acid juices bubble up from the earth's belly
stray dogs made of straw
melt on the window screen
bassoon frogs empty pond swollen flies
into the lap of my empty porch
green spring silence crumbles my window
beneath the cat's sleeping eye
the green ooze of lizards teeth
peels ants from the grey of rain trees
rust gathering aphids pry the mold
from my brain's hollow roots

Retrieval

Five young women
golden in their beauty
are gathered on two benches
adjacent to the pathway.

They giggle as they whisper;
they feed the multicolored
pigeons collected amidst
pools of sunlight scattered

by overhanging birches.
In their past lives they
were shoved, pushed and
imprisoned within the cells

of brothels, where they
were used, where they were
cursed by their users;
called whores, strumpets, tarts,

bawds and many other names
given to the despised.
But now, rescued and reclaimed,
they bask in their freedom,

having learned to ask for
their lives to be returned,
and found that though once lost,
now they are found and forgiven.

Creatures of the Black Lagoon

Just north of Panacea,
the DuPont family—
yes, those earth-enhancing
chemical producers—
built their Mediterranean style hotel
in spite of long humid summers,
hoards of mosquitoes
and water moccasins
where "the world's largest spring"
flows up from subterranean caverns
to disgorge the Wakulla River.

This broad cool ooze
of water flows below
Spanish moss draped cypresses,
while herons wade
and limpkins cower
camouflaged amongst cattails,
and water snails slide slowly
on one foot
like time itself,
while anhingas stretch out
their sodden wings to dry.

I don't know if
this DuPontian
fountain of youth
has elongated
anyone's life;
but that 100-year old alligator
grinning within his glass case
in that cool lobby—
an alligator that got fat

on catfish and Mallards—
might have given us an answer
if some trigger-happy fool
had not blasted him
into that great swamp in the sky.

Collateral Damage

Inadvertent is the word I spoke.
And though I did not consciously
intend self-absolution, that was
the path I had stumbled down accidentally.
For I did not know, at least
not without some doubt,
what would occur. I acted in good faith,

or so in retrospect I have come to believe
after some recumbent reflection when
the world was black and my thoughts
were dark enough to goad me
into uninvited reconsideration, when I would
have preferred to wrap myself within the dumb
and comatose abandonment of denial.

No, I disclaim all responsibility! My
sincerity is unassailable; my character witnesses
are legion. "These things happen," or
"It was unavoidable," are the explanations
suggested by those I choose to trust,
after long hours of grueling council
throughout which my purity of intent
was examined by experts—leaders in the field.

They all agreed that I was blameless,
even though deep in some fissure
hidden from consciousness, I knew.
What camouflage I wear! Though this
maze of syllables which displays and hides,
reveals and conceals is no more than
artifice—painted netting—no shroud so woven
can hide the carrion stench it binds.

Canticle to Myself

I have played the profligate; I have chosen
the path of the prodigal and run away
in search of ease—a route without pain.

My muscles have lost their tone, my mind
no longer thinks of anything but what I should
eat or drink. I care nothing for those who

have been abandoned, tortured, abused or
forgotten. I seek the way of mindless pleasure.
My inheritance—this earth—I willingly

trade for a pittance, as I sacrifice my children
to a ruined future, because I cannot bring
myself to labor. Instead, I have lived an

endless childhood basking within my sugar-
filled bliss. All I want is the taste of honey
on my tongue. Glowing praise is all I will

allow my ears to hear. I have spent my life
staring at mirrors. I cannot tolerate any image
but my own. I deny that I have been descending

for decades into the caves of darkness, into
the caverns of death. I have lost the key to
my soul among the slag heaps of the world.

Broken Steps

Within the smallest capillaries of my brain
where I hide from the staring of eyes,
I want very much to die,
to follow the tides of my mind's desire.
I strain to peel the taut tendons of my fingers
from their epoxy-strong grasp which holds me
like a scared lover within this life's hollow arms.

Blind nerves within these burning hands
desire to caress and fondle still
all the soft-skinned curves which wrap
the calcium hard, physical bones of this world.
My brain is not deceived by lying retinas.
I know that I am only a pitiful buffoon,
a pawn disclaiming his insufficient armor.

I have the driving will of a puppet.
A stinking jelly oozes from my spine
an ivory white string which I cannot bend straight.
Vertebrae spell out for me within unwanted phrases
the neglected epistles which laugh at human strength.
My muscles and ligaments do not control my feet;
they draw me into the rhythm of a crowded dance.

Some other hands, not mine, work my strings,
empty friends mock my broken steps
as I stutter through life's crushed sentences.
I always follow wide trails through the dark,
deep rutted paths, easy for the toes to cling to;
though I have a yellowing, outdated map
I sense the futility of my unpiloted voyages.

My searching mind keeps replaying old thoughts
which have the taste of cinnamon and sugar
coating the walls of their perfect spherical voids,
spices covering the emptiness of easy lies
which enwrap my silent tongue with pleasure
A sweet recipe hides the bitter stinging acid
which swallows the self-cursing of my mouth.

A festering pollution surrounds this earth
clinging like dry leaches to my old flesh,
wrapping me within a carious breath,
closing my eyestones to the sun,
stuffing my hollow ears with noise;
a saccharine syrup licks my white teeth
with the tongue of some counterfeit angel's voice.

Among the twisting fibers which lace
the nerve-stretched tunnels beneath my skull
I am deafened by cries to turn life loose,
this decaying corpse which strangles me.
I want to curl the fingers of my mind
around the gift of the gentle carpenter
who remakes the lives of the lonely dead.

Turning Radius

Whisperings

Small sounds
forgotten almost before they cease
tugging gently upon the fringes of
consciousness, beckon
with such intimate grace for
even the most tentative response—
some inconsequential gesture
to signify I'm not sure what.
They enter, sometimes
through the ear, but not always,
to glide precipitously along the periphery
of awareness,
not much more than a glimmer
on the horizon of cognition—
teasing seductively, but only mildly so,
they haunt me
suggesting that there really exists
that which is other
and holy.

Reims Rendezvous

Where his glowing presence came from
I do not know. An empty space
next to Mary that had been vacant, was
full now, of a persona—wings and robes
resplendent—a halo hovering above his head.
Later I would be told that he, this

beautifully handsome being, was Gabriel.
His subsiding wings fill my memory
with questions. How did he appear
out of nothing? How has the artist turned
his image into stone—stone that appears
to live, and speak, and overawe Mary,

at least initially, who seems overwhelmed
with surprise, and awed into silent
and everlasting stillness? Did Gabriel
already know how the story he was helping
to unfold would play out within this world
lost and fallen beyond chance of human

transformation or redemption? Could Mary
not but think that this glowing angel was part
of some cosmic dream too surreal for a mortal
to grasp and hold onto—one so limited
by flesh and blood? This message, the
expectation of it, the obligations and vast

consequences it encompassed—they were
ludicrous beyond belief. Instead of crying out
or deftly swooning, she retains her composure
in the face of this onslaught by a radiant

representative of eternity. She does not balk
or shrink within her inherent human frailty.

Instead, Mary offers the perfect response—
agreeing to play this proffered roll unsought.
She is innocent of the inevitable outcome, the
inexpressible and pain-filled agony that will
enshroud her humanness—invisible
for now within her future. Unencumbered

with such foreknowledge she becomes
humility itself, head slightly bowed, but with
her feet firmly planted on the solidity of earth,
and remaining in this world bounded by
chronological time and space, and the cruel hand
of death waiting—always waiting expectantly.

Her new task so fastened to—entwined within—
an imponderable responsibility, that could
so compress her soul that she would remain
gracefully immobilized as is her image,
adjacent to this entrance, to this place of sanctuary
and release. She is not so focused on

the immensity of what has been asked of her,
nor on that sly, slippery and slinking creature
who long ago set this world atilt within his lies.
She readies herself for the new life
that will soon form a nest, a temple within her.
Wrapped within her selfless devotion, and held by

the possibility of transformation it offered,
she remains in a world that has loosed its hold
on eternity, a world too long adrift—wafting
disconsolately within a polluted realm, a chaotic,

endless and barren expanse, shaped and eroded
by the centuries within our negligent misdirection.

This unnamed sculptor spoke truth;
enunciating with his chisel in stone
he formed and crafted a revelation—
an unflinching testimony, an affirmation—
one our minds will never be able
to fully disentangle or parse unaided.

Pushin God

I know,
I Know,
I keep on pushin God
right in your face.
"Lighten up," you say.
"Go skateboard on I-5"
you say.

Hey, you think
it's fun pushin God.
The retirement benefits
can't be beat,
but the pay is somethin awful,
an lately, pushers
have been gettin a bad rap.
Pushers are always
sticken their faces in yours
or mine,
pushin cigarettes
or whiskey
or life insurance
or some kinda pill
that'l cure whatever you got
that gives you pain.

Okay, okay
I won't push no more.
God don't need my pushin no more.
God's already there,
waitin for you to be just so tired
of what's makin you
wretched and pitiful.

Psalm

I can no longer feel the earth;
rebuild the fingers of my hands,
recover the soles of my feet,
touch my skin with many clouds.

I can no longer taste the water;
pry apart the crusted teeth,
empty my mouth of sand,
pull the thorns from my tongue.

I can no longer hear the wind;
chase away the crawling ants,
empty out the wax and pebbles,
wash my ears with small sounds.

I can no longer see the sky;
lift the clinging vine,
tear away the tendrils which bind,
separate the tight shut lids.

I can no longer see the light;
scrub the dust from my retinas,
polish the surface of the lens,
take the stones from my eyes.

On Wisdom

Ironic isn't it
that the tools of his trade were
used to hang him up. How
could a mere carpenter have
had the gall to let himself
be called a king? Clearly he
was a fool to attempt to change
the world with the likes of
fishermen, a tax collector and
others of no learning. They
were all lowborn;
their accomplishments
if you can call them that,
were of no account.

Ironic isn't it
that those uncouth laborers,
those uneducated men
were wiser than all kings, wiser
than all the greatest of thinkers
who came before
or after them. For they,
in their small and
insignificant ways helped to plant
and water and feed a kingdom
that the wise cannot enter
unless they choose to give up all
and become babies again.

Turning Radius

When God shifted direction
steered into a new heading
bringing him in line
approximating Abraham's plea,

how many new galaxies were formed
as he swung about?
How many black holes exhaled
within God's churning wake?

Or was it merely an almost imperceptible
nudging of the tiller
barely noticed
by angels swooping, laughing like gulls?

Mute Zechariah

No burning bush unwrapped flames before me,
no voice cumbered my mind or bid me
go barefoot beyond that holy veil
when I was chosen to offer incense unto you.
Fiery brightness caressed my fright;
your Gabriel waiting in ambush by the altar—
his sentences rattle still within my gourd-like skull—
his radiance pierced my stunned lids
unmasking images my eyes could not grasp.

Anyone but you would have asked,
demanded some sign to divide hallucination
from truth.   Little did I know the price,
little did I reckon the cost of this security I sought ,
no angelic light had twisted my eyeballs so before.
No otherworldly messenger had sought me out
until my turn tumbled me into your domain,
where all that brightness pounded numb my brain.

I had not divined that heaven's touch
could fill a heart with such bowel-wrenching dread.
Quivering through that endless hour,
as glowing embers of your love came to rest
upon my tongue; - that glib organ,
which bulged and fattened between my gray jaws,
I had not felt your wrath-filled kiss before—
it left me mute, dumb as a cold stone,
cast into that dark and echoing pool of light.

Such absurdity was I told—
sooner would I have held to myth,
or given in to sorcery and clamped my arms
about some base idol than take as genuine

this yarn, this fable spun before me as I froze.
Was it possible that impregnable Elizabeth,
old and barren as a scree covered slope,
breasts fallen down upon her stomach,
dried up inside and out, would conceive—
though surely no better wife could there ever be?

That she would bear fruit after drought, decades long;
such levity, though it might rend my belly
no longer taut, and empty my lungs of laughter,
could not gird with reason your heavenly prank.
Or better yet a demon wished to prick my heart,
that I might hemorrhage oceans of pain
and drown again, engulfed by myriad memories
of unanswered prayers, buried and almost forgotten,
from all those years when I pled with you,
for all the fasting and blood offerings
I spent upon your granite heart.

Elizabeth, groaning for the children
that never sprouted within her aging frame—
the little ones her aching flesh craved so,
more than silver or gold, more than life itself.

Oh yes, I smoldered, almost unable to breathe,
when the sign I sought smothered my tongue.
I will ever taste the bile, the humiliation,
while my family distracted by Elizabeth's rounded
and pear-like shape, abandoned me to silence,
to the mute imbecility I mimicked.
Their patronizing eyes caressed me with such pity,
they showered my sagging cheeks with kisses,
they shouted their pathetic platitudes at my face
burdening me with the weight of a deafness
I had not yet purchased.

Finally, her swollen womb expelled him,
spat him into his mother's weary arms,
and once I wrote his name my words returned.
My regained voice brought me little notice
once that wriggling miracle overwhelmed us.
Miracle after miracle spun me like a top;
my dizzy body revolved around that young,
soft-faced, swaddled, crying, sleeping cub—
woolly hair surrounding his round skull even at birth,
circling him with countenance wild and strange,
reminding me of beasts that haunt deserts
searching always for water, clear and cool.

You filled my heart with words I did not know;
poetry spilt from my mouth like honey,
sweet words bathing my tongue and lips,
pushing that nightmare, that caustic encounter,
deep into the dungeons of my dark night.
No, I could not grasp infinity
and draw its boundlessness into my heart.
The tide of love you crashed upon my shore
twirled me, left me thrashing in its wake;
I had not sense to float those waves
that pounded me, to give myself to you
without screaming madly in your face
my puny words of caution and mistrust.

Drawing Lesson

Lifting the pencil
I do not name the parts
making marks
I do not classify
erasing marks
I do not label
contours flow back and forth
without evaluation
features emerge
without criticism
as I face myself
I do not condemn
in each face I draw
I do not seek to perfect
I find the face of Jesus
holding me with his eyes
I see the face of God
welcoming, waiting.

Bearer

Down deep, below the Acanthus,
with their Art Nouveau blossoms
with their Hellenistic leaves,
flanking the Appian Way,

the catacombs inhale and exhale
through locked doors and barred gates.
Fresh air drifts downward, filling
each level, flowing from cubicula to

cubicula among the narrow passages
with their corpse-sized shelves,
beneath images of Jonah coughed up
by the whale-fish, below the rescued

lamb and where the good shepherd,
sandaled and strong, is bearing one
who had strayed and was lost
homeward, to the safety of the fold.

Addendum

We mourn
and then forget.

We are the scourge
that mines forests;
our extractions,
dismemberments,
our incidental brandings
of these soft hills
is only the preface
to what follows.

It began with
firewood for warmth,
poles for tents,
logs for cabins;
we meant no harm.
Then came loggers,
railroads,
overloaded trucks
to haul away the fallen.
The rains came,
hillsides slid,
erased saplings,
rerouted creeks.

We needed homes
furniture,
fuel,
pages to fill with poetry,
prayers
bills of lading.
We miss the passenger pigeon,

the Ivory-billed woodpecker,
the topsoil;
we meant no harm.

Now stumps,
gray and silent,
spread across hills
blackened and still.
Whatever we do
becomes enwrapped
with thorns,
becomes Golgotha—
a hymn to death.

Monotype

Maybe God does not use only clay
when forming each unique
and troublesome human that crawls or walks
upon this textured, living rock
we call our home. God's technology is
in no way bound by our limited perceptions
for what deity may do. Some, I am almost sure,
are sung into being, or danced,
while others are carved with steel chisels
before they are rubbed smooth with pumice.

I have begun to wonder, though of course
for now there is no certainty in my speculation,
if I was not printed into being on a small etching press
hidden in an alcove behind the drying rack.
Perhaps, beneath February's dark and brittle sky,
after morning prayers (listening to them of course)
and before moving on to some large canvas or
tapestry, God snatched up one small copper plate,
ink and a small brush, a much used fan blender
softened with age. Inks, some pale for the surface
and others, darker and richer for the depths below,
were pushed about upon that shining plate
yet uncut by acid or burin. It took but a microsecond
to complete the layered textures, lines and colors—

such is God's mastery. An angel, probably not Raphael
or Rembrandt, rather one unrecognized as significant within
our shallow history, ran this copper plate with the paper
that would be me through that small press. Perhaps the
plate once used was cleaned and used many times more
each time brushing, printing into being someone
unique—more burnt umber or quinacridone violet,

less cadmium orange. Some remnant marks from God's brush
remain visible when morning light slants westward
and the day has not yet been made too weary.

Psalm of Silence

Honied words flow from your lips
while the blood of the fallen
flows from your pen
to strike down
those whom would not be bowed.
O why can we no longer sing out high praises?
why must our words pander to fashion?
succumb to the trivialities
that surround us?
Our batons are all splintered
our strings are all broken
yet we would sing joyous praise to our Lord
even though all of heaven sleeps
restlessly now without our intricate
and captivating lullabies,
for the reeds of our clarinets have become
instruments of torture.
Woe come unto those who would ride high
on clouds of arrogant benevolence
smiling with their outward faces
while plotting our downfall
in their hearts.
Yet we would let the organ peal forth
in praise to our Lord
and raise our voices,
but cotton-like words now fill our scores
and only one endless melody
rings forth without variation—
to lull us into the sleep of the damned—
a strangling softness encroaches
allowing no air to enter our lungs
our musicians can no longer play and sing.
We would create songs palpitating with your presence,

but we are forbidden
by those that lord it over us
and condemn us for standing strong
in the heritage for which we were born and gifted.

Dark Canticle

When I should be resting
vast empty spaces of the earth
swallow my heart. The quiet

places swell, they rise up to steal
the breath from my lungs
and leave me empty and gasping.

Where can I find myself
within the endless caves of
my mind? Where is the water

that will fill me and the food
that will trap my hunger and
leave me satisfied and nourished.

As I dream the peoples of the earth
run about raging, they are filled
with the pain of their fathers,

overwhelmed with the sufferings of
their mothers. All sisters and brothers
have disappeared leaving them

deeply burdened and isolated.
Where is the shepherd who will
come searching within this wilderness?

To Return

Our day unwrapped itself with accustomed
laziness; we stretched slowly as the sun emerged
from within the thick tangle of limbs and leaves that
formed our bower. We yawned with delicious

and particular intention as we lifted our
arms skyward and unsheathed our sleeping souls
from the darkness and quiet offered to us
each night. There was no urgency, no uncertainty

in the garden. Monkeys chattered among the
branching green vaults above us and squirrels
debated among the leafy limbs. We ambled
along the slow path which unwound us towards

the stream. As we bathed the fishes darted and
played around our feet within the clarity
of pure and living water. We drank our fill and
plucked our favorites from the sagging crop

of fruit provided for us without any thought of
sweat or toil. Each awakening and each slumbering
was full, and generous and we gave it no thought;
for every day we were surrounded by flowers,

and fruits and trees of such variety as to
bewilder us only with the pleasure of it all. We
sipped nectar from flowers as did the humming birds;
we chirruped with the birds who also resided with us;

we stroked the soft and furry creatures and
buried our faces within the silkiness of their
benevolent embraces. We sought after nothing, strove
to gain nothing, for all was there for the taking—

enough for every creature. Although we celebrated
each day, as we gamboled beneath the sun and
stood silently in awe beneath the spread of myriad
stars, we were not always fully contented even

though we wanted for nothing, and could not imagine
anything else we might desire. Eventually doubts
slithered into our protected lives, twined about our
feet and sought to bring us down. Fruit from that

tree which was forbidden to us drew us closer
with some kind of mysterious and magnetic attraction
until we could think of nothing else. Our minds
so laden with curiosity filled our dreams with

richly hued bulbous orbs. We desired so much to
savor what we should not taste that when the serpent
enticed us closer to those branches drooping with
ripened fruit, we lost all remembrance of obedience.

We stuffed our mouths to overflowing with such
sweetness; yet we could not satisfy our cravings. Finally,
as the sky darkened into night, sticky juices clinging to
our skin we bedded down but did not soon give in

to sleep. Our minds raced. Questions without
number shredded the calm of night and kept us from
our usual bliss. We found that we knew many things,
some quite troubling, that were unknown to us before.

Within the light of morning as we unpacked the baggage
from our night, we came to see ourselves as naked;
we felt this need to hide within clothing. We did our
best to wrap ourselves within a tapestry of leaves lest

the gardener, the creator of all, should see our private
afflictions and send us hurtling into some great dungeon
of shame and self-loathing. These visions of self-
hatred scalded us until we burned all over—great

red blushes spreading like waves across the bodies
we had given so little thought to before we gorged
ourselves on what we could not ignore, once that
serpent—now become a venomous snake—

sunk his seductive, word filled barbs into our hearts.
We could no longer bear to be seen as we had been
made, instead we craved the shadows and searched
for dark places where we might hide within the

abyss that now began to stretch out between our future,
so laden now with anxious foreboding, and our simple
and uncluttered, lustrous past. Next, as we lied to our
maker, our creator, our once beloved protector, we

felt ourselves slide uncontrollably into hell on earth.
Those fearsome cherubim drove us from the sacred grove,
but in truth we had already departed once we failed
to seek out mercy, to plead for forgiveness. Surely

we would have been scooped up into a warm and generous
embrace if it had not been for the pride that came with
all the knowing with which our minds were now
encumbered. We could not bring ourselves to cry

out in supplication, for in our greed to know, and then
know even more, we had lost that inner knowledge of
love that had always sustained us. As soon as our
feet crossed that border into the land of self;

once the garden was behind us we began to blame
the other. I castigated her and she glared back with
those rage filled eyes stabbing me with such disdain. It was
as if the very fabric of our existence had been rent

from end to end. This separation spread throughout
our lives and even though we might cling to each other
in our fear or need, we never again could claim to
know each other, or even care to understand each

other as we had before we gorged upon that damnable
sweetness hidden within a smile of lies. You know
the rest (for you have lived it) you know how we struggled
and bled and fought each other within that realm of

our own making. Yes we had vast knowledge, we were
king and queen of our own domain, but it was such
a miserly and barren world we had shaped within
the toil and turbulence, within our blighted rule.

You live as we did, still separated, still apart, not knowing
how genuine love untutored by pride, or greed, or an
intimate fixation on the self can be. And although we
weep within our solos, our monologues of pain

and grief, we can no longer sing in harmony as we
once did. Our pathetic attempts to bring true unison
to our voices reminds us, when we can tear ourselves away
from our mirrors, of this loveless drought. We glimpse

within the shards of our brokenness flickering fragments
of what was, what still could be. And now, after long
dissolute lives we cry out to our creator. We know,
while impaled still by doubt that we are loved, and cared

for. We, both she and I, know down deep below our aching limbs within the turmoil of our lives, that when we offer to sacrifice our knowledge completely, that we will be gladly welcomed back, allowed once more to return.

Spirits of The Earth

Shaman

a scalpel of feathers
bound together with tendons
cuts through the flesh
the green of the earth
searching out the barbed cancer

angels of mercy
empty their quivers of arrows
pregnant with hybrid seed
into the caves of the city
filled with buttons and uniforms
filled with the bones of children

cities of sand
your hourglasses lie strangled
their necks are all broken
their skulls are all empty
the bloodcrusted fingers
have found their haven of death

shaman wrapped in your mask of feathers
searching the womb of the mountain
scraping the granite lichen
the flint blade fills small pouches
feathers of dove
feathers of indigo bunting
wings of dragonflies
web of the spider
to wrap the manshaped stones
fingers tasting the humus
fingers griping the bloodroot

only the shaman's chanting of legends
revives the stiff corpses
songs entombed in the valleys
revives the solitude that lived
early on the earth
when blood pulsed
in the veins of the mountain
when stones were still liquid
before man sunk his foot
into the mud of the delta
before the rib of the moon
was split from the earth's maw

a porcupine flung into the night
barbed quills
forcing holes into the night's cloth
stars blooming
in the blackness without eyes
icicles of light sweeping down
cold fingers unfolding the leaves
of bloodroot and stonecrop

owls chase night through the trees
wise men of morning worship the sun
dog howls warn of the stranger to come
eyes forget to count
the seasons of the moon
eyes of the night
read only the spreading rings
floating within gasoline puddles

the stalks of straw
as they fall into patterns in fields
count out the formulas
the paths that the future will follow

in the minds of the seekers
prophecies cry out
from the cracked skin of sidewalks
ghosts of the future
wrapped in wires
ride on the waves
lost in the fog of moonlight
burrowing moles suffocate
within cities between rivers

the flight of the pigeon and starling
carry the burden of unfulfilled omens
fingers of tallow
reach up from the pavement
looking for promises
in the shrines of the alleys
the incense of tires burning in dump heaps
the flames of the sacrifice
lost within furnaces

revelations lost between columns
wrapped among ears
in the closets of newspapers
the scattering of crows on the grave
the weeping flight of doves
funeral rites are buried in laughter
hysterical stones of the forest
cry out in pain
the land of machines buries her woodlands

octopus tentacles
connect the stumps of tongues
a concert of monotone screaming
mouths drowning
in the hollows beneath eyelids

the hands of the shaman
grow restless on the drum
the grey hands of the shaman are dying
the dust of sourwood and bloodroot
falls through his fingers
his thoughts have no heirs
his language is dying
his eyes have no pupils
the words which he speaks no longer have ears
his eyes search
the eyes of the sons of the village
their sockets are vacant
their minds drift through green smoke
their heads are all wrapped within wires

who will sew them together
before the eyes of the tribes
scatter their paths in the wind

River

Ambassador
groaning with the spoils
of the land
beer cans of tribute
are caught in shadows
that ride your river's train
what happened
to the white duck's call

priest
laden with offerings
the ocean's stomach rumbles
your wine is poison
flowing to the altar
what happened
to the silver scaled salmon

friend
with many inland arms
clinging to the lonely mountains
are you dying
will you go away
will you follow the red men's ghost

Cherokee

My eyelids are opened
by the sun's warm tongue
walking the lost trails
of the Cherokee

ferns are no longer folded
by silent moccasins
the yellow smoke of greeting
is lost among green shadows
where the river bends its elbow
beneath the mountains
muscled shoulders

between green
kneecaps of ridges
flooded into Cherokee silence
my hands dig
into the moss barked forest
my fingernails sink
into the mass of red veins

tangled within hemlock roots
I find a young brave
hidden in the eyes of a fawn

do not burn me with your eyes
my hands were lost
in searching

Red Winter Ghosts

Crazy fire water powered warriors
medicine eagles dance
gnawing the red wind's blankets

stupid pig-toed bison stampede

painted hawks hunt the snow
for dreamer ghosts

tree boats
slaughtered river moccasins
walk the crowfoot pass

squaw trappers
suck the broken bitterroot pipe
quiet broken arrow horses
Missouri ice
lists you among the dead

Coyote Knows

You may believe that you are hidden,
unnoticed beneath the cascara tree
among the western waterleaf and saxifrage.
Your inhalations and exhalations,
although they are relaxed and shallow,
ride the wind, as does the scent
of the Solomon's Seal crushed beneath your left boot.
Coyote knows the soft perfume of your bath soap,
your deodorant—the minty tang of your toothpaste.
They gently declare themselves within the currents,
the rivers of air that wash over you
broadcasting to every observant nose
that you ate eggs, sausage and oatmeal with huckleberries
sweetened by locust blossom honey, and
that your choice in tea was Earl Grey.
You are always seen, heard and known
by those that encircle you with their lives;
although unseen, they are not oblivious.

The Collector

I am a collector of rainbows;
the soft lightening of
the mocking bird and wood thrush
which dances through the leaves
shaking the light which lies sleeping
within the spider's hammock.

I am a collector of smiles;
the dim thunder of
the mountain's round stones and pebbles
which rumble cautiously among
the smooth whispers of the night
gliding through the trout's mica pools.

I am a collector of laughter;
the bubbling winds of
sounds which ripple from your eyes
like the sunlight's verses
which drip from the stone cup
of the waterfall's song.

Unwrap The Moon

unravel the leaves
which hold the sun
let it float down
behind the next ridge

follow the silver
eyes of warblers
lost among thin notes
hung upon clouds

collect webs of dew
tangled within
the vine's tendrils
copy signatures of spiders
dancing in the coals

unwrap the moon
held within laurel
unlock your own hands
let them feel deep
into the heart of the mountain

Wind River

from the top of Wyoming
the vision of your glacial birth
has stolen my eyes
the wind swallows its own sound
I have hidden my cold ears
beneath a loose rock

your snow bleached blankets
gather warm footprints
that I leave in silence
among running hoof prints
of bighorn sheep
embossed on the scattered snow

your stream's fingers
bleed with refuse of scoured mountains
polished intestinal rock
suspension of glacial flour
white milk-water
between ice jawed boulders
within snow wrapped skunk's breath
crushed petals of sky pilot
caught by the purple wind
I find my lost hands
wrapped with sheep sorrel
a lemon wind tastes the sky

I search within your stone fields
the grey scent of rock pica enfolds me
within their hidden haystacks
with hummingbirds lost among flowers
I harvest the greenness
of this empty backbone

pushed up among hawk shadows
feathers caught in a cloud's throat
down below the white hail
broken ice stripes
float across the lake's shallow eye
retinas of sunken rock
caught between my soft toes
cold dreams buried among beads
strung with the eyes of golden trout
a water mirror stretched taut
distorting the brittle straightness
of lodge pole forests
careful elk slip unnoticed
through the evening window of your sky
into the valley's moist pockets

among the fallen toes of a cliff
left uncovered by the sun
I bury myself deeply
within a willow bog
thin roots of bluebell and rose crown
woven into a thick cape
keep mosquitoes from my shoulders
moose and mule deer lap cool water
from the bowl within my hands
river you pull your waters from me
leaving my mouth full of gravel

your waters have fallen from the mountains
river of the wind
fallen to flow among slow cattle
thin water snake among buttes
within a hollow sandbox of ranches

Facing the Light

Without fanfare
disk of moon fades into haze,
slides silently
into distant waves,
blue now
as sun mixes with water.

Gulls preen
sip fresh water
flowing from the land;
always vigilant
their feet slapping wet sand
as they scurry,
scatter.

Expectant,
waiting,
without impatience,
and mostly quiet,
they congregate facing eastward;
facing the source,
facing the light.

Paths

Paths to and from the garden
lead me in and out, back
and forth among thoughts that

bloom and roots that ripple
beneath my feet, collecting
minerals, drawing up nourishment

from firm earth that forms
stems and stalks, spreads leaves,
weaves flowers and threads

seeds that fill all light
with mirth and groaning, beneath
a canopy both vaporous and bright.

Mixed Media

Cloud wrapped geese
swim seas of rain that dive deep
to drench me, fill my pockets
with chilled hands.
My boots squish and crunch;
gravel mixed with worms
escaped from saturated earth
held in place by roots sunk downward
by grass, by saxifrage and hellebore.
A canopy of warmth spread by sun
spawns forests of streams
ablaze with spring-green trees,
ash, maple and skeletal birch.
Busy chickadees pester the air
peck and pull at fringes of a veil
sundered by screaming jets,
here then gone,
scouring peace from this holy ground.
My boots' flow joins a trickle of songs,
my prune wrinkled toes emerge
with squirrels' chatter
to converse with moss, vanilla leaf,
stonecrop and arnica

The Cartographer's Dilemma

Below drooping firs, limbs dripping
as clouds are trapped between
red cedars and hemlocks,
I follow this dotted line that leads me
past a grove of Devil's Walking Sticks
not indicated on my map.
Outstretched and thorn encrusted branches
pluck at the edges of my awareness.
My steps lead me in and out of myself,
my mind full of brown contour lines
and blue watercourses draining
these folded ridges interrupted
by shrill squeaks flung out by rock picas
at intruders into their dominions of stone.
No signs are posted, no fences or boundary markers
give me notice that I am nearing a frontier.
I find myself stumbling across boundaries invisible.
Trip wires alert patrols of blue jays,
cascades of abusive shouting and vituperation
engulf me, throw me into retreat;
or a rattle path-side, but not clearly heard,
awakens me; or a deep throated, rasping growl
that began imperceptibly
now thunders through my ears.
All maps, no matter the scale, are useless
when so many layered territories overlap—
their boundaries in constant flux.
I find myself sitting on a stranger's bench,
or I find some friend is stepping on my ego
or I have trodden upon my companion's sacred treasure
unaware.

Moonset Coda

Snow patches,
stitched quilt-like
between dark, emptiness of grass
and ghosting sidewalks,
glow in the pale fire
of a slivered moon, just
a crescent,
dangling.

Dark firs stretch
into a yawning sky, still punctuated
with remnant stars,
as fissures of sunlight intrude
bringing night's paragraph closure,
release.

Nature's Continuum

The Birth

Glassy eyeballs of the sun
wheat yellow blood drippings
hang out stretched from snakes tongues
bait to tease bilingual spiders
weaving heavy black lined webs
imitating carbon copies of trees
hung from highway bill boards
dragonflies divide the lake
with a shoestring
unlaced from a bittern's nest
among the caterpillar hills
rippling between the sun's knuckles
the moon unfolds from within
a crumpled gum wrapper

Into Day

Early in the day when live oak
trees stretch out into daylight,
their long limbs draped with

Spanish moss, and when Mockingbirds
send out their solos into the
still and quiet air, I climb into my

canoe and paddle across the flatness
of the lake. As green shores recede
behind me I glide into morning

before the sun creeps upward, before
insects drift, like miniature dreams,
until snatched and swallowed.

Already the air is thick with
moisture rising from the brown,
cypress dyed water collected in

this shallow bowl surrounded by
low, green hills. As I near the
deep center I slip my T-shirt over

my head, then lower myself until
I am immersed completely into
the cool darkness. After inhaling

I let myself sink, descend into this
alien world until my feet tangle
with water weed and soft semi-liquid

earth. I stay at the bottom until
I have no choice but to rise, lungs
straining, back into the world of

air and sky and slim blue herons
lazily flapping their wings in slow
motion towards some unknown

destination. I descend and ascend
until the brightness of the sun heats
the day towards steam and discomfort.

Reluctantly, I return shoreward
uncertain, not knowing what this day
will offer, which path I will follow,

or where I will be when darkness,
humidity and mosquitoes pursue me
and I seek respite within sleep.

Four Trees

Came down on that windy night
(I'm not sure which one), winds
pushed and pulled at those tall
cedars that stretched upwards from

the steep-sided gully. First a cedar
snapped and fell towards the north.
Its weighty solo shoved against its
leafless neighbor, a maple rooted

in the soft soil of a narrow creek's
bed; it gave way. This duet of trees
leaned into another cedar until
it tilted, tugged on its roots until

they loosed their grasp on rain sodden
soil. All three forming a trio within
the grip of gravitational urgency
came to rest against a fourth and

more obdurate cedar which resisted
the urge to lie prone upon the earth.
So it did not fall. Instead it embraced
a massive Douglas Fir which was

more firmly rooted. For weeks this
quartet remained suspended until
the men with chain saws came. It
did not take them long in that din

of gasoline engines to bring them
all down to recline in death.

Wild Flowers

Herbicide settles on green
spring grass, settles on dandelions,
red clover, killing.

Rotating blades bite into hard clay
soil roils upward, dust chokes wind,
lifts, drifts, surrenders, sinks.

Eight cubic yards of sandy loam
dress a gravel bank too steep
and indigestible for biting blades.

Rain turns clay to paste, smothers
dust; regurgitated roots, grass stalks,
weeds interweave blades, rain, muscles.

Scattered seeds pepper dry earth—
raked, smoothed, pampered, watered
with skeptical expectation.

Green intrusions rearrange dust,
pattern steep bank and flat below,
unfamiliar stalks and leaves emerge.

Stuttering cadences of sprinkler percussion
web evening air, spilling water
across parchment, unilluminated.

One orange California poppy precedes,
enters afternoon heat and glare,
unfolds optimistic forecasts.

Natural blossoms, reintroduced, cultivated;
sown upon this ungainly plot that never
ceased raising up bountiful grass, weeds.

Granite Fingers

hardness
surface of stone

balcony
attached to no house

collections
feathers of light

circles
drawn by a hawk
grey
against grey
in a wet sky

odor
rabbit's blood
clinging
to the weasel's clenched teeth

eyes
granite fingers

antennae
polished by rain
rising
above the earth's skin

Mountain

Mountain
between protruding lungs
I was almost lost
among footprints

among wasp baited traps
hidden beneath rhododendron stubble

grass tufts have struggled
through the crumpled
crumbled skull

scratched boulders of bone chips
litter the balding scalp

scars of blueberries
cling to empty sockets
of wind rotted stones
that lick the clouds

clear cold blood
bubbles from unhealed wounds
to mingle with my sweat
in the warm throated crevasses
of snake scaled gullies

Pebble Children

Old man
sitting by the dark pool's eye
sanding stones
making round egg pebbles

young sparrows in his hair
having learned to fly
pull worms from his ears
before they dissolve into earth

the nearsighted pool
gathers her pebble children
and pulls shadows
from the sun's branches
lining her nest

When The Hawk's Flight is Forgotten

Beetles roll out of dark brown eyes
interrupting the conversations,
of invisible friends
drinking tea from plastic cups,
imaginary banquets;
blackberries wrapped with thorns,
may apples
and dandelion wine,
gallons of ice cream melting away
in the hot throat of summer
until some August,
or September morning
lowers its brick curtains
to lock away the summer mind.

Trees walk about the hill's wind
stopping only
before the dreamless eye,
that searches for snails
and looks for the door
to a salamander's wet home,
beneath rocks crayfish claws
tickling the tongue,
spiders dividing up the sky
for hopscotch and other games,
daytime ghosts playing tag
in the tall field's grass,
frogs yelling at the moon
which has fallen into their pond
cracking its mirror.
The eyes of summer remain
only until lost among the
sheep in blue denim.

Willows wash their hair in the sunlight,
of a still pond,
leaves fallen from a tree's library
are checked out by the wind;
leaving short messages,
a thin veined handwriting of poems and plays,
which merges with eyes and ears
until washed away,
on a school's stone altar,
when the hawk's flight is forgotten
among the chalk clouds of a blackboard.

Forest of Dreams

I wake from dreaming—
visions of stumps
covering every hill, every valley,
rank after silvery rank
from here to eternity—
to find my head cushioned
by small needles.
My nostrils inhale
a multi-textured aroma—
leaf mould, compost of cedar and maple,
bracken and lichen.
An eager mosquito, in search of breakfast
frolics by my ear;
avoiding fluttering fingers
it advances and retreats
as other sounds trickle into awareness—
chattering, rushing water
gurgles into one ear and out the other.

Now that I can see above larkspur and waterleaf
as my arms push me upward against gravity
I face a large stump, moss covered and dark,
surrounded by towhees and wrens
scratching and darting
within speckled light;
they bring me back to the stump's eyes
which stare at me with such comprehension
and uncanny knowing.
My lips move, forming words,
but these syllables I speak do not come
from within my brain;
my feet too begin to move—
I find myself upright, pulsing with promises

of energy and light—
singing and dancing fills every cell within me
and I must move

I must surge forward and back
responding to a rhythm
reverberating within my skull;
I follow a melody, quick and light
enunciating words with precision
from some language I do not know—
neither my tongue
nor my feet hesitate or stumble—

Who am I?
Why have I never danced this way before?

Bighorn

three bighorn sheep
guard a frozen circular silence
trapped between cold rock
stone hard pastures
scattered flatness above
a dying trickle
blood of a snowfield
absorbed by cotton clouds
red phantoms lost
above the reseeding sun
three bighorn sheep
run with a black wind
crushing the mountains
small quiet flowered fingers
with nights pounding hooves

Drouth

Baking soda dunes
nests of ping pong balls
eggs incubating
in sockets of lifeless dust
hatch machine smooth
iron bellied owls

infra-red eyes
to harvest rubber mice
hovering the night's black carpet

synthetic soil unwatered
dried crust without drouth

plastic dahlias listening
tasting the metallic drone
of the spring driven bee.

Hayden Pond, Rain, November 11

A windless net of rain
Surrounds the pond
with its grey siege.
For two days now
the clouds have filled my eyes.
No sunlight has unwrapped
the dull foil which seals this broth.
A sandy bottom filters a savory recipe
of perch, pickerel, and bluegill,
oak leaves and maple replace the bay.
Through long hours of counting
a relentless rhythm hugs my roof
hypnotizing the muscles which hold my eyes.
I have begun to retreat
into the hibernation of my cottage;
with the fish I sink deeply,
burrowing beneath my quilts
hoping to evade the coming cold.

Hayden Pond, October 8

If I had a boat,
you would find me
at the center of the pond,
circling with the wind,
wrapped in its chaotic dance.

It is a holiday,
and yet the water is empty,
boats lie strewn along the shore
like empty tortoise shells,
overturned.

I would be dancing on the wind's song
following the crazy laughing voice
scattered by the sky's bellows,
taunting too, the earthbound waves.

Even the dry leaves
rattle silently through the sky,
sketching their wingless flight
across the sky's almost empty sheet,
orange dots peppering the blue.

As I have no boat,
I will imagine the wind
crashing through the waves' rhythms
as they sweep the pond.

Goodbye Sunrise

The brittle pinch
of the blue jay's scream
warns the white tuft
on the buck's rump
to wave goodbye
to the hard knuckled mountain
plastered with the yellow mustard
of sunrise

blinded
I search for my eyes
among the stream pebbles
my hands imitating
the sharp spiked
sparrow's claws
which grasp the morning
like a chemist

Listen to The Earth

Wood Nymph

You are clothed
in an island of soft green

your lungs breathe
only moss cooled air

filtering the dark
blue smoke of night
spider plants
webbed in macramé nets
hang from your ceilings

dreaming of green forests
you sleep
nestled among quiet ferns

Drones

Drones hum
accompanied by the wind
rocks have fallen
to cover the spring
the copper colored pony is afraid
but all four horses stare
the rock is uncomfortable
but I play on the grass blades
tunes of the long dead wind
the cicada rejoice
for the world is lost
the music of the grass
is lost on the wind

The Garden

It isn't always clear which to uproot
and which to leave,
for young sprouts so resemble one another.
Clarity comes only as stems rise up
and leaves emerge, unfurl,
as solitary buds, spikes, racemes, umbels form
leading us to awareness, revelation.

Even then assurance remains elusive
for blackberries grasp so much and with such strength;
stick weed evidences admirable persistence;
dandelions spread their happy-faced abundance
with such abandon;
fireweed has that pioneering spirit.

Are any of these qualities
less admirable than beauty
when all will succumb to cold or draught
and crumble into dust?

Revealing

Until the goats arrived, and stepped
curiously from the back of the
beat-up old Ford truck, the landscape

lacked specific shape and clarity.
Those five goats were efficient. After
several trips around the perimeter

and sorties into the outer fringes of
that tangle of blackberries, salal and
cascaras, they began to nibble.

Hour by hour they ate; slowly a slightly
rumpled landscape emerged, rising upwards
towards the northern line of fence.

Only the taller shrubs and trees escaped
those voracious jaws and teeth. The goats
are gone, and it is quieter now that
so much green has been erased.

Preservation

Nature collectors
wrap eagles with cellophane
and rubber bands
bats are dried in ovens
and hung in closets
stuffed elephants
are stacked in empty warehouses
snails are frozen
into the neat squares
of ice cube trays
butterflies
are pasted like stamps
on envelopes and sent to zoos
lizards caught by children
are pickled for biology labs
salt water aquariums
are filled with plastic fiddler crabs
so the oceans can be emptied
and mined
robins caught by cats
are put in sandwich bags
and taken to school
glove compartments
are stuffed with beetles
lions are folded
and stacked neatly in linen closets
hatboxes are filled
with rattlesnakes and chickens
national parks
are leased to circuses
tourist's movie cameras
capture what is left of wildness
all of the animals are silenced
only the clouds are screaming

After Burning

Wet now
with summer's burning
long past

singed forests
scared and fragile
inhaling ashen breaths
expelling asthmatic
lamentations

where needles lie heavy
on pathways
now seldom travelled

blackened trunks, limbs
lace sky to earth
twine wind
to brittle silences
ensnaring melodies unsung
unheard

Raising Up Dwellings

We build our houses on land
that was once tree covered
with fir, with hemlock
with maple and alder.
We scrape the land
with machines fed on diesel;
gone are the waterleaf,
the saxifrage and windflowers,
the thimbleberries and salal—
there is room for them no more.
Into trenches dug with backhoes
we pour our ribbons of concrete;
creating barriers that impede
earthworms, ants, moles and
others who dwell beneath the
surface. Our trees, reformed now—
smoother and straighter—
are raised to make walls.
Power tools hum and whine
as we saw and nail and enclose
our plumb and planar palaces.
So much death—is it all essential
as we shape and bound
our spaces for living?

Resin Enough

Slash pines,
gouged, scared
and drained of sap
for turpentine
kept many rural families
solvent
in Wakula County,
where low clay hills
sink holes and tree farms
give way to scrub oak
palmetto and swamp.

Slash pines,
fast growing
and straight-trunked,
most of them labeled S.J.P.C.,
flank highways for
miles along those flat
endless roads
to Sopchoppy,
to Bloxham.

Slash pines
spread their needles
like brown hay
upon shade covered earth;
needles that could be
stuffed into metal toys,
cars or airplanes,
then torched
to simulate catastrophe.

Slash pines
with their ladder of limbs
drawimg young boys
up and up
to that silent expanse
of sky
and wind
where no parent
would think to go.

Wind Walking

Wind–pushed along
the winding arcs of
Taylor's Ferry Road,

I avoid sporadic
shimmering puddles
punctuated by raindrops,
gathered along
the asphalt edge.

Several early cars
drone past—headlights
slicing darkness.
Weighted clouds spill
their dark contents

as the sun struggles
within this
inclement conspiracy.

Angels' Rest

On this stone peninsula
surrounded by wind,
vision is clearest behind closed lids
when sunlight massages back,
neck and shoulders
releasing congested traffic,
erasing gridlock,
disentangling collisions
held tight by nerves and muscles.

Air currents deliver invitations—
yellow biscuit root,
purple salal berries,
a grey jay's silhouette—
collected from gnarled roots,
rocks, fissures and unseen wings
to entice the heart.

Hiking Above Coyote Wall

Maples, leaves turning yellow
and orange—gathered in clusters
near the now empty streambeds

and in hollows where small bogs
form in springtime—rustle in the
breeze. Dark and menacing clouds

to the west threaten us with rain.
in this open expanse, golden now
after weeks without rain, an

alternating pattern of sloping ground
and deep cliff-bordered ravines
divide this hillside, forcing trails

into labyrinthine twists and turns.
From above, among boulders
surrounded by seed pods and

skeletons of arrowroot balsam,
Oregon spreads its panoramic
splendor out across the far bank

of the Columbia. Lower slopes
are spread with fields and orchards
folding and unfolding our lives;

further up evergreens crowd
along ridge tops and above clear
cuts. Higher still, the stone steps of

Mt. Hood, mostly grey now before
early snow, rise into an angry
turmoil shrouding the summit. On

the highways below drivers ignore
the onset of rainstorm and wind as
they hurry towards some destination

that magnetically draws them closer.

Listen to the Earth

Newscasters cry wolf
to keep us from changing channels.

A dark blue pick-up truck
is parked in the rushing ocher water
of Marshall Park.
Tryon Creek, a roaring tumble
of earthen froth, widens to lick
bases of swing sets and slides.

Large maples,
brought down by December wind,
spread water wide
across what once was lawn.
Downstream, across a concrete court,
closer to the northernmost hoop,
sprawls a fallen cedar.

Not far away, in Scio, a girl
gone to get the mail is swept away
as rivers change channels,
shove humans into shelters.

We paved everything,
balanced our homes
on hills of mud;
we thought we were in control.

Rainy Ridge

It was one more cloudy morning,
another in a series of overcast beginnings.
Our trail took us uphill through
columns of evergreens a-drip with
remnant clouds tangled around

their uppermost branches. As we
climbed we glimpsed Wahtum Lake
from open places above boulder fields.
We passed Turks Cap Lilies, Lupines,
Penstemons, Indian Paint Brushes

blooming brightly beneath the clouds
along the Rainy Ridge Trail. We could
see the snowy base of Mount Hood
from the bare and rocky spine between
infillings of clouds. We lost track of

time as we walked further into this
new day and new place. At some point,
it is difficult in retrospect to determine
when, the trail began to slope downward;
instead of firs and hemlocks,

Monkey Puzzle trees rose around us,
enveloping us within a symphony of
strange sounding birdcalls and languid
aromas. When we reached an open meadow,
with small huts scattered about near

a lakeshore, we knew we were lost and
clueless. There were no inhabitants about.
We found a dugout canoe-like craft, along

with two paddles. It beckoned to us,
invited us to set out across this unknown

water. After what seemed hours we saw
a small island with scattered trees and smoke
rose lazily from behind a gentle slope of land.
The island seemed to call to us, so we
altered course from aimlessness to purpose

and soon reached a graveled shore. There
was another canoe pulled up away from
the gentle lap of wavelets, so we pulled our
borrowed dugout further in and stowed
the paddles within the craft. It was then

that an unexpected weariness settled upon us.
We could go no further; what energy we
had possessed departed and left us lethargic—
unable to move. We must have lain down,
spread ourselves out atop the grass along

the shore and slept. But when we awoke,
it was to gathering darkness. Mount Hood
rose confident in its strength, bathed
in evening light, but it was now to the north,
and we were not beside Wahtum Lake.

Tomlike Mountain

Yesterday,
when we set out, uphill
on the anthill trail along the ridge,
with no map. We missed
the trail to Tomlike Mountain.
It was only when we reached
a viewpoint and the clouds
shifted long enough that we
could see our goal off to the
north at the end of a ridge
we had not noticed. Somewhat
dispirited we turned around,
retraced our steps to the junction.

We decided to follow the Herman
Creek trail to see where it would lead.
We had descended only a short
distance when we met a hiker,
better prepared than we were;
he let us check his map. We
saw the error of our way and
continued until the Herman Creek Trail
dropped eastward
down towards Mud Lake.

A fainter, but visible trail continued
along the ridge top toward the treeless
summit we sought. We followed
this winding track over rocks and
among scrubby evergreens
until we stopped for a late lunch
amid a pile of stone slabs.
We watched as clouds tickled and licked

the mountain tops nearby. We did
not reach the peak. We had wearied
ourselves too much with that
false move, nor did we want to face
that long logging road in darkness.

War and Art

Shiloh

Each night after stars have risen
above his battlefield, and taps has
ceased its lonely and unaccompanied
mourning, General Grant walks
into the night. You cannot see
him stepping deftly among the dead;
only the glowing tip of his cigar marks
his presence. He always goes alone;
he tells us he walks out among the ghosts
newly born, to apologize for all the stupidity
that leads to war. A general who sends
young men out to die cannot sleep
until he walks the bloody hills that
he has painted; a vast bone yard that
can never be fully purged—made clean.

A New History Lesson

When all the wars have ceased
and the dead have been buried
to breathe no more, it is the winners who lose.
They are the ones who must invent
the lies they will tell their children,
lies of glory in the face of death.
What is left of the defeated remnants
will have no voice as their mourning
fades into dust, disperses like smoke,
and no one will believe them as they sink
into their cocoon of sorrow and pain.

The earth draws these waves of death,
carries them gently into itself,
and holds them in the stone caverns
deep beneath the pavement and soil we see.
Some future day, when the victors,
grown fat and lazy least expect it,
this hidden past will erupt and circle
through cities and towns, spreading
a new song full of truth and light,
that can no longer be covered over.
History will be rewritten to tell
the truth, and all voices will be heard.

Blessed

Blessed are the investors
(they are the soul of the nation),
they walk the straight and narrow bottom line.

Blessed are the entrepreneurs
(as they drive their sleek Mercedes)
who gamble with our pensions.

Blessed are the brokers and advisors
(whose past performance is not predictive)
who dance to the market's tune.

Blessed are the portfolio managers
(minimum investment $5,000)
with their oracular, insider vision.

Blessed are the corporate CEOs
(with their multi-million dollar bonuses)
who downsize our sisters and brothers.

Blessed are the capitalists
(and their assault on the earth)
with their throw away workers.

Blessed are the cool headed accountants
(in their pin-stripes and ties)
who tally the profits and losses,
who tally profits and losses.

Canticle of the Dead

Where are all the leaders of the lands?
They have fled in silence knowing
that their answers are selfish lies.

All of them have sold themselves—
made themselves slaves to the rich,
idle men and women who promise

a taste of heaven. Their voices are hollow
like the empty tombs they have fashioned
as receptacles for their bones. The powerful

care only about this day; they have
abandoned the poor, disregarded the sick
and thrown out the orphaned children

to fend for themselves among the beasts
that were once men and women. All
humanity is sacrificed for gold—for trinkets

and baubles that cannot satisfy. How can you
know all these things and not weep? You
must take a different path. Abandon the

well-traveled highways that lead to the abyss.
They all lead to the black hole of death—
eternal emptiness without respite.

Carbolic Canticle

Purge the operating theater with ammonia,
with bleach, with your own caustic brew,
sterilize all surfaces; scrape away scabs,

Sand down the scars, cauterize all raw ends
of limbs; unravel all sutures. Expand pain
by whatever means, by jostling or pummeling,

By pounding with a rubber mallet. Abrade every
surface, raise welts, increase the decibel level
to a tumultuous, raucous and irritating climax.

Drive away all sanity, all rational thought—spin,
swirl, jerk all appendages in frantic, manic imitation
of disjointed marionettes, of electrocuted cats

Frenzied, fur smoking, reeking, yowling, lurching,
tumbling drunkenly for all eternity until all energy
all life, all willpower is extinct, extracted, until

Breathing ceases completely and the flat line
trails on forever.

On Days of Remembrance

After the dust, from the last armored personnel
carrier has settled, and the smoke from ruined
buildings has ceased to rise, when quiet has descended,

the carrion eaters will come. Men, women
and children will creep about removing anything
of value from the dead and mostly dead.

Watches, cigarette lighters, money, wearable
boots will be stuffed into pockets or canvas bags.
After the wedding rings are removed, the teeth

with gold fillings pried loose, and the nearby sand
sifted for unnoticed spare change or bullets, the
buzzards descend and stray dogs, tails between

their legs, will sniff, gnaw, and fight with each other
for their share of the spoils. Later, when the best
morsels are gone, the rats will arrive, scurrying

from corpse to corpse; they will crawl through
ribcages and skulls until all flesh is devoured.
In this faraway place where so many lives have been

snuffed; after the sand has drifted to cover
scattered bones and tattered remnants of
uniforms, truth and memory will fade. What was

in reality a small, and sordid, and terrifying event
will become something grand, or at least be counted
as unavoidable. Remember this when the soldiers

march past on parade, recall these images when
those who send others off to die make great speeches
or talk of "national security." Broken families,

children without parents, parents without sons
or daughters know that the scars of war are permanent—
some wounds never cease to bleed—never heal.

Muscle-bound

Michelangelo is to blame.
He may not have started the craze
for pulsing pectorals, or bulging biceps
bigger than a normal man's leg,
but he pushed that seam-straining
envelope until every muscle flexed.
Superman, Batman and Spiderman
have nothing on Jonah or Daniel—
not to mention that Cumaean Sibyl—
and those other hefty Sistine hunks.
This God, and Adam too perhaps, after he was
energized by almost touching digits,
could juggle planets and heft the universe
without breaking into a sweat.

Linocut with Arrowroot Balsam

Stark white flowers stretch
petals into an inky black, spreading
themselves across mould-made paper

with deckled edges—evidencing a
tactile personality. Claw-like
sepals, curling leaves and bits of stem

emerge into view as white and
black explanations of figure and
ground present clarifying

suggestions about light and space. After
the lengthy process of transferring image
to linoleum has taken place outside

our scope of observation, and
the sharp gouge has excavated an
array of small pits and troughs,

something visual has been formed,
printed, matted and framed—an
unfurling of a person unseen and seen.

Grinding The Stone

It is the way of the lithographer
to mark upon this crystalline purity,
this hard white surface
cut cold from deep within
earth's lightless core.
Black crayon traces its greasy track
upon the eye, approximating, though crudely,
something seen or unseen,
something taken from those solid mirages
we choose to embrace or disengage
depending on—depending on
which uncertainties we gather
into some semblance of coherence.

After this image negotiates
some compromise resembling closure;
once the proof is perfect
obsessively inspected, reworked, corrected,
then multiplied exactly
within the separation of waters parted
as ink kisses grease. Then—
then comes a time of purification,
embracing solvents stinking and cancerous
as ink is purged, image voided—cancelled—
leaving that pale evanescent ghost.

After the sprinkling of grit
without ceremony, as the levigator
spins its hesychastic praise
of steel on stone, the lithographer
seeks within this timeless task
to make the rough places plain.
This honing down, this carnival

of expurgation is the way of the stone—
imagination breathes itself
into visibility, is readily accepted
and willingly released. This
unselfish collaboration, layer after layer,
tends imperceptibly towards something
close to nothingness—towards spirit.

Andy Warhol's Doesn't Live Here Any More

You got more than your share
with your brash multi-paneled prints,
Campbell's soup cans and Brillo boxes
rudely grabbing our eyes, trying to pull them
from our startled sockets.
The factory, its wild art making—
parties with crowds of crazies—
is legendary, like your endless movies
that no doubt put your bored persona
into a deep and coma-like sleep.
The failed murder attempt made us
sympathetic momentarily. Then you
shocked us all by dying unexpectedly
on the operating table, though
long after your fifteen minutes
of fame had already elapsed.
No doubt God enjoyed your antics;
you are still beloved, wild hair,
bland oral eccentricity and all.

Drawing with ink

requires almost total commitment,
for intense black ink is an
assertive medium resistant

to evasion or correction,
so mistakes remain to confess
the miscalculations or limitations—

all of the drawer's imperfections.
So why not use graphite?
(we choose not to speak any

more of pencils). Graphite is a
noble medium with enhanced
potential for blending, but black

blacks remain elusive and drawing
seldom flows so felicitously
without the flexible fibers

unwinding lines and shapes
from within a brush.

Goya's Black Paintings

Bats wheeling, darting,
plucking hapless insects
from within inky blackness
brushed on thickly;
ridges of dried paint
follow the arcing movement
of the painter's arm and hand.
Witches, warlocks
and other creatures of the night
cling to the flatness of walls and ceiling.
Their familiars creep from caverns
within the painter's mind,
the spawn of his isolation—
his misbegotten children—
bent on escaping
from the tattered fragments
of his soul.

Listen

Listen
as the poet spreads his smooth
and bitter words into a vast darkness
coating your hunger
with sugar and brine.

Extend your tongue
into night,
lick up the evanescent scent
that lingers
within sparks
and currents that flow
as he strings his twisting cage
of molten, shimmering glass
and ice-dark wrought iron
to tease and taunt
the endless yearnings inside you.

Allow yourself to become entangled;
do not struggle against
his intravenous flow of syllables.

Be carried away
drift, float, waft
within this onslaught—
its rhythmic inflections—
that lifts you up,
that releases you from the chains
you have fashioned.
Unbind your imprisoned heart.

Listen.

Wood-fired Torsi

For Mark Terry

Born of fire
torn from the earth
scorched and twisted
is this second birth.

Our stubborn geography
beneath supple skin
reveals scars without
uncertainties within.

Torsi rise and fall,
release each breath,
folding tangled mysteries
within silent death.

Splintered wood ash
embraces pliant clay
to enclose, obscure,
transform, display.

Born of fire
torn from the earth
scorched and twisted
is this second birth.

Acknowledgements

Thank you to the editors of the following publications in which many of these poems first appeared:

Ann Arbor Review: "Well of Morning"

A New Song: "Mute Zechariah"

Cardinal Poetry Quarterly: "Beneath the Cat's Sleeping Eye"

Christianity and Literature Journal and in the book *Imago Dei: Poems from Christianity and Literature:* "Turning Radius"

East River Review: "Cherokee"

Facing the Light: The Art of Douglas Campbell and *Oblique Voices Press:* "To Return" and "Facing The Light"

Flint Hills Review: "Tide Searchers"

Gryphon: "The Death"

Halcyon Days: "The Collector" and "Hayden Pond, October 8th"

Harbinger Asylum: "Unwrap The Moon" and "Psalm"

Indiana Voice Journal: "Father's Words," "Broken Steps," and "Hayden Pond, Rain, November 11"

John Milton Magazine: "Turning Around"

Nature's Gifts: Anthology of Prose and Poetry Celebrating Nature and Our Natural World: "Angel's Rest" and "Erosion"

Nothing, No One. Nowhere: "Carnival," "Linocut with Arrowroot Balsam," and "Andy Warhol Doesn't Live Here Any More"

Off the Coast: "Coyote Knows"

Pebble Lake Review: "Facing The Light"

RiverSedge: "Creatures of the Black Lagoon" and "Collateral Damage"

The Dakotah: "After Burning" and "Moonset Coda"

The Eleventh Transmission: "Goya's Black Paintings"

The Ides of March: "Shiloh"

The Path: A Literary Magazine: "Enunciation, Retrieval," "Mixed Media," "Wind Walking," and "Wood Fired Torsi, For Mary Terry"

The Rockhurst Review: a fine arts journal: "The Cartographer's Dilemma"

The Wineskin: "Tide Walker"

This: A Serial Review: "Addendum"

Tiny Moments edited by David Pring-Mill: "Cloth"

TWJ Magazine: "Pushin God," "On Wisdom," and "Bearer"

University of Tampa Review: "The Birth"

Windhover: A Journal of Christian Literature: "Collateral Damage," "Whisperings," Reims Rendezvous," "Drawing Lesson," "To Return," "Paths," and "Grinding the Stone"

Other books by Douglas G. Campbell

Seeing: When Art and Faith Intersect. (Lanham, Maryland: University Press of America, 2002).

Facing the Light: The Art of Douglas Campbell. (Portland, Oregon: Oblique Voices Press, 2012)

Parktails. (Eugene, Oregon: Wipf and Stock Publishers, 2012)

www.ingramcontent.com/pod-product-compliance
Lightning Source LLC
Chambersburg PA
CBHW021152020426
42331CB00003B/23